The
Marriage Cup
and the Covenant

The
Marriage Cup
and the Covenant

Pastor Raymond D. Horry, D.DIV.

_____

The most authentic book, except for the Bible, ever inspired by God on the subjects of marriage, divorce and remarriage.

The Marriage Cup and the Covenant

Copyright © 2023

Pastor Raymond D. Horry, D.DIV.

Publisher's Ref Code 12g445.44rt-1222

This book is dedicated to my wife, Kathy and my children, Raymond Jr, Raynard and Witney.

Your support has meant the world to me!

I would also like to thank:

The Ark of Safety Christian Church

Family and the Administrative Staff

My mother, Ruth and my sisters, Alfie, Cynthia and Chris Denise

Dr. John A. and Rev. Diana P. Cherry

Bishop Charles E. and Mrs. Gladys Wallace

Eric Battle, who was instrumental in the first publication of this book.

Contents

Foreword

My husband and I share an inside joke. When an item we want to buy costs more than my husband seems willing to pay, I look over at him and ask, "You can't pay the 5.00?" Regardless of the price, he always wonders if the investment is worth it.

But as my husband and I both know, when it comes to investing in your marriage, there is no cost too high. Getting married is one of the most important decisions you can make, second only to your decision to receive Christ. This is why I am so happy my husband wrote this book. This book will prove to be a worthwhile investment.

As you will learn, the enemy tries to destroy families by diverting those closest to us. However, when we follow the proper order of God (recognizing the man as the head, the woman as the submitted helpmate and the children in obedience), the enemy's plan is destroyed.

I have seen my husband triumph, fail, struggle and go into this place I call 'the cave'. He never stays down there too long. When Mr. Raymond D. Horry comes out, he pushes forward in his commitment to do the work of the Lord. It gives me comfort and makes me feel secure. Since I know my husband is in complete compliance with God's will for our lives, I want to do everything I can to be an incubator for the dreams and desires of his heart.

It took work to get our marriage to this point. My husband and I made a deliberate decision to learn about the marriage covenant. I'm so glad we did. And I promise the same blessings we enjoy are available to all believers. The blessings are in the cup.

Minister Kathy D. Horry

Chapter One
Understanding the Cup

S peaking in a definitive tone that depicted authority, Mother Jones bellowed: "Do you know about the marriage cup? Has anyone ever told you why God created marriage? Do you know what it takes to stay married? No? Well, child, don't you think it's about time you learned?"

These questions marked the beginning of Mother Jones' marriage-cup talk. On any given Sunday at my former church in Washington D.C., Mother Beatrice Jones would take a young woman by the hand, sit her down and lecture her about the marriage cup. Though much time has passed, I can still hear her strong, steady words:

"Baby," Mother Jones would say as she held the hand of the young woman sitting beside her, "you certainly are growing up, aren't you? I see the way you prance around here. You remind me of myself when I was your age," she would say with a small chuckle.

"Anyway, I reckon it won't be too long before one of these young men around here is trying to put a ring on that finger of yours." Then, with a serious tone and a stern look, the wise, old mother would advise, "Now, you listen to me, honey. Before you walk down the aisle, you better make sure you know what you are getting yourself into. Marriage isn't anything to play with. I may be old, but thank the Lord I ain't blind. I see the way you and that

Johnson boy look at each other. I see how you two carry on even when the preacher is up. Everybody knows your courtship is getting serious. But, baby, before you take that boy's ring, I want you to think about something.

Do you remember in the Bible what Jesus was praying in the Garden of Gethsemane? Do you remember what He told His Father? He said, "Father, let this cup pass from me." The cup Jesus was talking about was the commitment He had to fulfill at Calvary.

Now, don't you go tellin' folks that Mother Jones said getting married is like being crucified, even though some days it may feel like it is. All I'm saying is that some cups are heavy. Before you pick them up, you need to make sure you have the strength to swallow what's inside.

You see, you're used to sipping from the dating cup. The dating cup is fun; it gives you something sweet on your tongue and cool on your lips. But, when you start sippin' from the marriage cup, some days you're gonna burn that little tongue of yours. You gonna taste some bitter with the sweet. If you ain't ready for it, you need to let that cup pass on by."

My Assignment

Every time I heard the marriage-cup talk, something in my spirit would begin to stir. Although I was still young in the ministry, I could feel that God wanted to use me in the same way in which He used Mother Jones. My purpose was to teach young and old alike about the divine institution of marriage.

My purpose crystallized as I became more aware of the brokenness all around me. My city was filled with broken homes and broken lives. As I looked at the scores of hurting people, I didn't need Marvin to ask: *What's Going On?* I already knew what was going on; I knew that the brokenness was symptomatic of a break in the institution of marriage. Moreover, I knew that our communities would remain broken until the institution of marriage took its rightful place in the fabric of society.

This conviction stayed with me. Over the next twenty years of my life, I worked diligently to become an expert on the topic of marriage and divorce. I read Christian and secular books on the subject. I considered what theologists, as well as psychologists and sociologists, had to say on this subject. I was committed to doing whatever I needed to do, so I could fully understand God's plan for husbands and wives.

Through all the ups and downs of my life, through the wilderness experiences of my life, people came and went, and situations came and went, but this call never left me. When I tried to put the mantle down and follow popular religious trends like the church growth fad or the economic development movement, I could hear God say, "Son, that's not your ministry. You don't get to choose the message; I already chose the message for you. So keep on studying the covenant."

It's Time

Then, one Sunday morning, I was scheduled to preach the 8:00 a.m. service at my church in St. Louis, Missouri. I served as the assistant pastor, and on that particular Sunday, the senior pastor was away.

As I was preparing for church, the Holy Spirit spoke to me in a powerful way. The Spirit told me, "Now is the time. It's time to come out of the wilderness of preparation and start teaching the people about the cup and the covenant." That was the moment when God released me into my divine destiny.

When I stood up to preach that morning, I was determined to do just as God instructed. I announced to the congregation I would be teaching a lesson on marriage and divorce. As I began to speak, I was nervous and afraid. I wasn't afraid because I doubted my message (I knew what I was saying was true), but I was fearful of the crowd's reaction. I didn't know how they would respond to my message. Since I wasn't planning on pulling any punches, I knew my message was about to hit some people hard. I knew some folks were about to get convicted, and strongholds were about to be knocked down.

Towards the end of my lesson, I stood there like a prize fighter waiting for the devil to hit back. But, to my amazement, I looked out over the crowd and saw that chains had been broken and people had been set free. I saw the heavy burden of ignorance being lifted up off the people as they began to understand what God required of them in their roles as husbands and wives. There was not a single angry face in the congregation.

The people were hungry for more teaching. I was shocked. The people of God wanted to learn the principles of building a godly, stable union. They wanted to know how to stave off a divorce and stay in the will of God. The people of God were ready for the whole truth and nothing but the truth. In fact, the preacher who was scheduled to preach the 11:00 a.m. service demanded I continue with my teaching. It was evident I had the divorce demon on the run!

The Struggle Continues

The divorce demon is stubborn. It continues to plague the people of God at alarming rates. Every day its mission becomes easier as the amount of false teaching and misinformation increases. Worldly philosophies constantly undermine biblical teaching.

For example, modern marriage counselors regularly advise people that living together before marriage is a good idea. They claim pre-marital cohabitation gauges compatibility and can be a trial run for a successful marriage. Read what a popular online advice column offers on this subject:

> *If you want a better chance of having your relationship last, it's a good idea to live with your partner before marriage. This way, you will be able to tell whether you are compatible or not. It would be a shame to get married and discover that in such close quarters, day in and day out, your partner doesn't look so good anymore.*
>
> *People are busy making a good impression while dating. It's natural in this phase to downplay bad habits and less-than-stellar traits. It's easier to look good. Once you share a home and both let your hair down, that's when you will find out if you are a good mix. And if you're not, it's less traumatic to part ways after living together than going through a divorce.*

What nonsense! Living together isn't a marriage. Living together is just shacking up. You don't learn anything about your girlfriend or boyfriend by shacking up; all you learn is how to live outside the will of God. Yet, people are taking the advice of misguided experts and following their counsel. Have you ever considered where all their advice has left us? I'll show you.

The divorce rate in America for first marriages is 41%.

The divorce rate in America for second marriages is 60%.

The divorce rate in America for third marriages is 73%.

Clearly, our society is in bad shape. Traditional marriage is under a heavy assault by the devil and his messengers of deception. As a pastor, I see the results of the devil's handiwork each and every day. I counsel Christians who are suffering because their marital arrangements are outside of God's plan. Some of the people I talk to are legally married to one person but still under a covenantal relationship with their ex. This unfortunate arrangement developed because they hired a lawyer and received a legal divorce, but God never granted them a spiritual divorce. Take note: no lawyer in the world can put asunder what God has put together, and no court on earth can break the spiritual union of marriage.

Scripture teaches that there are only three conditions wherein God grants His children a spiritual divorce and releases them from their wedding vows. They are:

I. Adultery - Matthew 5:32

But I tell you that anyone who divorces his wife, except for marital unfaithfulness, causes her to become an adulteress, and anyone who marries the divorced woman commits adultery.

II. Physical Abuse - Malachi 2:16

"I hate divorce," says the LORD God of Israel, "and I hate a man's covering himself with violence as well as with his garment," says the LORD Almighty. "So guard yourself, and your spirit, and do not break faith."

III. Abandonment - 1 Corinthians 7:12-16

To the rest, I say this (I, not the Lord): If any brother has a wife who is not a believer and she is willing to live with him, he must not divorce her. [13] And if a woman has a husband who is not a believer and he is willing to live with her, she must not divorce him. [14] For the unbelieving husband has been sanctified through his wife and the unbelieving wife has been sanctified through her believing husband.

8

Otherwise, your children would be unclean, but as it is, they are holy. [15] But if the unbeliever leaves, let him do so. A believing man or woman is not bound in such circumstances; God has called us to live in peace. [16] How do you know, wife, whether you will save your husband? Or, how do you know, husband, whether you will save your wife?

Although I will offer a more detailed explanation of the principle of breaking the covenant in chapter two, suffice it to say, at this juncture, if you are a Christian who has divorced for reasons outside of these three, then in the eyes of God, you are still married. I know this may come as a shock, but it's true! Sure, your divorce may have been valid according to natural law, but it's invalid according to God's Law. After your unlawful divorce, instead of living happily ever after, you end up living a lie. Instead of being free to date and remarry, God still sees you as bound to that man or woman you are trying to forget. Once you understand marriage is a spiritual union first and a natural union second, then you will see why God is the only one who can release you from your bond. If God didn't release you, but you released yourself, **your only option for your future is sin or celibacy.**

Not only do I counsel those who are still spiritually tied to their ex, I see many people who feel trapped in bad, dysfunctional marriages. One reason people get trapped in bad marriages is that they become lonely and desperate and marry the wrong person. In their haste, they settle for someone to whom they are neither physically nor spiritually attracted.

Regarding this first point, as you read this book, you will discover I not only recognize the spiritual aspect of marriage, but I also acknowledge the natural side of marriage. I don't believe in, nor do I teach, spooky spirituality. Spooky spirituality is the misappropriation of spiritual principles in situations in that God has declared part of the natural order.

As you are choosing your mate, never forget that marriage is for the flesh. Marriage is a part of the natural order. It was given to natural beings. According to the natural rules and impulses governing marriage, you should be physically and mentally attracted to the person with whom you enter into a covenant relationship. If you marry out of desperation and bind yourself to someone unattractive or unappealing to you (*unappealing because of their attitude or features*), then you will be permanently tied to someone who does not measure up. Being in covenant with a man or woman who doesn't turn you on is a recipe for disaster. You'll see. One day someone who is your type will walk by, and you will have to fight back your attraction to the eye candy in front of you.

Unfortunately, many people are unsuccessful in this fight and end up breaking the covenant and going after what they should have waited for in the first place. The Bible says in 1 Samuel 16:7 that *man looks at the outward*. So, it is natural for you to seek after someone who is appealing to your eye.

While physical attraction is important, you must also be equally yoked in a spiritual sense. Don't marry Tall Tyrone or Kinky Kim just because they turn your flesh on. If they don't share your values and love for Christ, then the joy they bring to your body won't make up for the destruction they will bring to your soul. Christians who get married just because they have the sex-itch must remember that after you scratch it, the marriage continues. After the love-making is over, the life-making continues. Therefore, you need to make sure that the yoke is stronger than your lust.

Nonetheless, if we say *I do* to someone whom we should have let pass by, then we shouldn't be surprised when we don't live happily ever after. Nor do we have any business getting upset with God. He didn't do it - we did it. And instead of lying in the bed, we have made for ourselves, some of us rush out of the marriage. This is the reason so many marriages end in divorce.

I wrote this book because I want to help people overcome all of the problems, issues, misconceptions and fallacies I just outlined. I want to help those in bad marriages and those in unequally yoked marriages. I want to prevent people from rushing into marriage and strengthen people who have already rushed into bad marriages. I want to release people from their confusion.

One day, as I was thinking out loud about the book, my wife suggested I title the book: *The Marriage Cup and the Covenant.* When she said that, I thought to myself: That's it; now, all I have to do is explain to people what's in the cup.

I believe knowledge is power. The more you know about marriage, the more stable your marriage will become. The reason many marriages fall apart is that so many people go blindly into marriage. They start sipping from the cup but are completely unaware of what's in the cup. If people took the time to find out what's in the marriage cup before picking it up, then perhaps, the divorce rate would not be so astronomically high. I believe if some of us knew what we were about to drink, we would have taken a thoughtful step back and reconsidered whether we really wanted the experience. Maybe we would have reexamined the person with whom we were about to share the cup.

But, even though we are already married and already committed, it's not too late to study what's in the cup. Knowing what's in the cup, even as you drink from it, can help save your marriage.

Too many Christian couples are willing to throw in the towel when problems arise. This is because they have the false assumption that marriage shouldn't be hard and it shouldn't take as much work as it does.

This is why you need to know what's in the cup. If you know what is in the cup, the good, the bad, and the ugly, then instead of being surprised at all the bumps in the road, perhaps you will find the strength to hang in there and ride it out.

And once you learn what's in the cup and the rules that govern marriage, you need not worry about those rules changing. Society may change, but marriage and its rules are not up for revision. According to God, marriage is just as old-fashioned today as it ever was. I often use a sports analogy to drive home this point.

The game of basketball was invented by Dr. James Naismith. Early in 1891, Dr. Naismith came up with all the rules governing the game. He defined what a foul was. He defined what was permissible and impermissible. He said if you hit the arm of a player taking a shot, then that player is entitled to take two free throws from the foul line. Although Dr. Naismith came up with these rules almost 120 years ago - guess what? The rules still stand today. The rules that Dr. Naismith came up with way back in 1891 are still in place. They have covered the game through the careers of Wilt Chamberlain, Kareem Abdul-Jabbar, Michael Jordan, Kobe Bryant, Lebron James and John Wall. The rules are still the rules.

The same is true for marriage; the rules are still the rules. Once you learn and master the rules, you'll be able to ride out any storm and outlast any problem. When God created the marriage cup, He created it to last. With these truths in tow, let's take a look inside the cup.

Chapter Two

Commitment in the Cup

If you were to survey ten people at random and ask them to identify the one issue causing most of the destruction and misery in our society, nine-out-of-ten respondents would most likely cite issues such as poverty, crime, diseases, drugs and so on. While all of these issues are ruining lives, I believe the epidemic ruining most lives is divorce. That's right; divorce is public enemy number one.

One reason it is true is that divorce affects more people than all those other social ills combined. Experts estimate that in 2009 there were 1.3 million drug addicts in the U.S. The total number of victims of violent crime was 3.4 million. The total number of homeless persons was 3.5 million.

But in 2009, the total number of Americans who had their lives ravaged by the onslaught of divorce stood at 25 million people. What a sobering statistic! And like drug addiction, crime and homelessness, divorce kills, steals and destroys. Anyone who doubts this truth has completely underestimated the pain and anguish a broken union causes for women, men and children. Those who are considering divorce would do well to realize, among other things, divorce destroys self and self-identity.

Divorce Destroys Identity

[But] whosoever committeth adultery with a woman lacketh understanding: he [that] doeth it destroyeth his own soul. Proverbs 6:32

The certainty of this verse is undeniable; breaking your marriage vows is a form of self-destruction. It is true in adultery, and it is also true in the case of an unjustified divorce. When a believer divorces their spouse without precise biblical justification, they rip asunder that which God has put together. Moreover, they tear apart the spiritual oneness that is at the center of the marriage covenant.

As you might imagine, this kind of crude and brutal ripping never leaves a clean break. When you rip asunder the marriage covenant, you also rip away a piece of your soul, you rip away a piece of your heart, and you rip away all of the shared hopes and dreams you and your spouse have built together during the course of your marriage. So the truth is, when you unlawfully walk out of your marriage, you don't find yourself - you lose yourself. Before you rush into divorce, you need to understand that a biblically invalid divorce will destroy your self-identity.

When God created us, He placed within us certain drives and instincts that we are wired to satisfy. Men have certain God-given instincts, and women have certain God-given instincts. These instincts, or drives, make us who we are and form our nature and identity.

A man's identity is a protector and provider. A man's nature causes him to seek out a wife whom he can emotionally, physically and spiritually protect. Men have an internal drive to be the head of their own little clan. Any man, who is a real man, wants to be a leader, a husband and a provider. This makes him who he is. It's the reason he goes to school and gets a job; it's the reason he spends hours at the gym trying to build muscle; it's the reason behind most of his activities-he's trying to attract a mate so he can care for her. Being a provider and protector is at the core of manhood.

Likewise, the identity of a woman is rooted in her drive to be a wife and a helpmate. A woman's identity includes the instinct to nurture and bring beauty and meaning to her family. No amount of career success or dating can satisfy a woman's internal desire to be a wife. A woman wants to be loved and able to give love to her own family.

So, when divorce occurs, it means that neither man nor woman can continue to walk in the identities for which they were created. Their identities get destroyed in the mess of divorce. A man, who wants to be a protector and provider, suddenly has no one to protect or provide for; he has lost his identity. A woman, who wants to love and nurture, suddenly has no one to love and nurture; she has lost her identity.

Not only does an unlawful divorce rob you of your identity, but it is also important to point out that remarrying someone else won't bring back your identity. This is because your identity will always be tied to the person with whom you are spiritually bonded. A man who remarries after an unlawful divorce doesn't regain his identity as a protector and provider, but now, his only identity is of an adulterer, nothing more and nothing less. The identity he craves is still back with the one he left behind. During an unlawful divorce, our identity remains tied to our spouse even after we have left.

Of course, the devil tries to hide this from us when we are making up our minds to divorce. The enemy tries to hide this dirty secret and put a cover over the pain we are about to inflict upon ourselves by giving up our identity through a divorce. I am determined to keep people from being deceived; my job is to pull the covers off of the pain. I want every married believer to know how much divorce hurts. I want married believers to know giving up your identity is never easy. When you can no longer do that which you were created to do, it will cause confusion and regret. When I explain this principle to young men, I sometimes use the experience of basketball legend Michael Jordan to illustrate my point.

Sports fans will recall Michael Jordan first retired from professional basketball on October 6, 1993. In his 1998 autobiography, *For the Love of the Game*, Jordan wrote he had been preparing for retirement as early as the summer of 1992. He alluded to the fact his exhaustion due to the Dream Team run in the 1992 Olympics, coupled with mourning the death of his father, robbed him of his drive to play the game and led him to decide to retire. As Jordan soon found out, when you walk away from your purpose and give up your identity (in his case, his identity as an all-star basketball player), you end up making a painful, regrettable mistake. The magnitude of Jordan's mistake was made evident in the way he struggled during his retirement.

First, he had a failed stint with the Chicago White Sox. (Playing baseball couldn't give Jordan his purpose back because Jordan's identity wasn't tied to baseball, it was tied to basketball.) Next, he purportedly got into severe gambling trouble and difficulty at home. And finally, when he decided to return to the NBA, he had an erratic record, never quite capturing his previous greatness. In fact, some sports writers suggest, even to this day, Jordan has never fully recovered emotionally and mentally from the time when he foolishly sacrificed who he was because of the momentary pressures of life.

The correlation between Jordan's experience and the experience of Christians who are considering an illegitimate divorce is this: just as the loss of identity hurt Jordan, the loss of your identity as a husband or a wife is also going to hurt you. It hurts so much some people never recover from the pain. Some become so impacted by the pain that in a desperate attempt to numb themselves, they turn to drugs, alcohol, promiscuity and the like.

Therefore, it's easy to see how divorce and its aftermath rip apart the very fabric of our society. Show me a society where people are angry, bitter, frustrated and hurt, and I will show you a society where the divorce rate is on the rise. Moreover, show me a society where the divorce rate is on the rise, and I'll show you a society where sickness, disease, and illness are on the rise. The online periodical, *Divorce Life Online*, offers this observation:

> *Studies have shown a positive correlation between divorce and incidence rates of stroke, cancer, parasitic diseases, acute infectious diseases, and digestive and respiratory illnesses. It was even shown that married cancer patients are more likely to recover than cancer patients who were divorced. Divorced men have lower life expectancies than married men.*

What a staggering depiction of the damage that divorce afflicts the individual. But, as you will discover in the next section, divorce doesn't limit itself to hurting men and women; divorce is an equal opportunity destroyer that also hurts children.

Divorce Destroys Families and Children

The physical and emotional toll divorce exacts on husbands and wives is just the beginning; the devastation of divorce extends to the whole family. Take a look at what researchers at *Divorce Life Online* have found when studying the effects of divorce on children:

> *The grieving process that follows any loss can be viewed in a divorce as well. The dissolution of a marriage is a death of sorts, and those going through a divorce grieve. Depression and anxiety often follow on the heels of a divorce and affect all parties involved, including the children of the union.*

The best indicator of teen suicide is parental divorce.

College attendance is 60% lower for children of divorce than those from intact homes.

In ratings by parents and teachers on peer relationships, hostility toward adults, withdrawal, and aggression, children whose parents were divorced performed more poorly than children from homes that consisted of both parents.

So when you take a step back and begin to see divorce for what it really is, a brutal storm of destruction, then you can see why God hates divorce. God hates divorce because of what it does to men. God hates divorce because of what it does to women. He hates divorce because of what it does to children. God hates divorce because of what it has done to the world He created.

The Divine Commitment in the Marriage Cup

God's hatred for divorce and the destruction it causes is the reason He fortified marriage with a divine spiritual bond. By fortifying marriage with a spiritual covenant, God is fighting back against the evil winds of divorce. The spiritual fortification of marriage gives husband and wife something that will keep them together long after the honeymoon has ended. The spiritual covenant holds strong, even when the love has died down, and the interaction has gone sour.

You see, God knew that men are whimsical and are attracted to newness. It is not uncommon for a man to find a woman, fall in love, get married, and then suddenly feel as though he is missing out. Instead of focusing on the positive, he will look at his wife and see only her faults.

I know some women disagree. They will say, "Not my husband; he's too wise for that." But, if David and Solomon, the wisest men who ever lived, let their desire for new loves and new wives wreak havoc in their lives, then what makes you think your man is any different? The reality is if God had not fortified marriage, then the lure of newness would also destroy your husband. The only thing that may have kept your husband from looking outside of your marriage is the divine commitment.

God also knows that women are whimsical in their own way. There are many women who are simply in love with being in love. As long as they feel loved, all is well. But, the moment the feeling of being loved begins to wane, they look for that feeling from other sources outside of their relationship.

And for these reasons, God fortified marriage with a commitment that could not be broken by our whimsical natures. He gave marriage a commitment stronger than any other commitment, except for salvation. It is stronger than anger, disgust, hurt, boredom, bitterness, attraction, and all the other emotional and mental challenges standing against it. In fact, the spiritual bond in the marriage cup is so potent some of us find it hard to swallow and difficult to stomach. Some people even try to water it down and dilute it by seeking out the kind of false teaching that will give them permission to do what they want to do. But remember, by fortifying marriage with a spiritual bond, God is blessing your relationship with stability and security.

Think about how insecure you would feel if your marriage relied on your ability to keep emotions high and the thrill strong. What if your marriage rested on your ability to constantly please, satisfy, excite and intrigue your mate? Under these conditions, you would live under the constant fear that if you did anything wrong or said anything wrong, then your spouse would break the covenant and seek fulfillment elsewhere. What a nightmare marriage would be. Husbands and wives would be in a constant state of anxiety, never being able to rest in their relationship or feel free to be themselves.

But fortunately, God put rules in place. These rules take the pressure off of us and remove all the guesswork of staying married. The rules don't deny peace; they provide peace. That's why I challenge every married believer to fully understand what the rules for divorce are. When you know the rules, you know what behavior qualifies as covenant-threatening and what behavior is not covenant-threatening. Now, on to a full examination of the rules.

God's Rules Concerning Divorce

When I first started teaching about marriage and divorce, I was amazed so many people were in the dark. But, I knew their bewilderment was not God's fault. Make no mistake; the Bible is clear in its doctrine and precepts. Therefore, the only reason Christians are in the dark about marriage and divorce is that too many pastors and preachers refuse to teach the truth about marriage and divorce. Perhaps this is because they, themselves, don't know the rules. Maybe they never took the time to study the scripture to find out. Who knows? At any rate, it's time to end the ignorance and come to light.

But before I outline the rules, let me reiterate the point that divorce, even when justified, should never be considered a happy solution. Even when divorce is spiritually permissible, the best option is to work through your problems. You may think this sounds overly optimistic, but have you ever read Matthew 19:26?

> *But Jesus beheld [them], and said unto them,*
> *with men this is impossible; but with God all*
> *things are possible.*

Saving your marriage may not be possible for you to accomplish on your own, but with God's help, all things are possible. I tell people all the time; never say there is no hope or that a situation or relationship is dead and gone. It may seem dead and smell dead, but God is the only one who can pronounce something dead.

Moreover, if it is dead, God still has the power to reverse death and turn around dead situations. This was His message to Ezekiel:

> *The hand of the LORD was upon me, and carried me out in the spirit of the LORD, and set me down in the midst of the valley which [was] full of bones, and caused me to pass by them round about: and, behold, [there were] very many in the open valley; and, lo, [they were] very dry. And He said unto me, Son of man, can these bones live? And I answered, O Lord GOD, thou knowest. Again he said unto me, Prophesy upon these bones, and say unto them, O ye dry bones, hear the word of the LORD. Thus saith the Lord GOD unto these bones; Behold, I will cause breath to enter into you, and ye shall live.* Ezekiel 37:1

What an awesome God! The same God who, under certain conditions, grants divorce is also the one who can keep us from divorce. Remember Jude 1:24?

> *Now unto him that is able to keep you from falling, and to present [you] faultless before the presence of his glory with exceeding joy.*

These are necessary preliminary points. I would hate to rush into the rules concerning divorce without first pausing to acknowledge what pleases God most. It troubles my spirit anytime I encounter teaching about divorce that does not give heed to the healing power of Jesus Christ. So, if you are rushing to read the rules to see if the divorce you want is permissible, slow down. Yes, God has authorized us to divorce under certain conditions, but He would rather want us to fix our broken relationships. He would rather see us give Him a chance to breathe life back into the dryness of our dead intimacy and dead trust.

When both husband and wife have a sincere desire for God to work, then God can perform miracles. Pride must be set aside, and the record of past wrongs has to be set aside. The table must be set for the redemptive power of God to fill your cup and to put the sweetness back in a sour union.

It may be difficult to comprehend, but with a willing heart and God's help, the same man whose presence and voice irritated you can once again become your best friend. The same woman, who hurt you deeply and rained misery down on you, can be transformed into your strongest advocate and a reliable confidant. All God requires of us is we bring ourselves to the point of humble surrender. He knows how to heal us from there.

> *If my people, which are called by my name, shall humble themselves, and pray, and seek my face, and turn from their wicked ways; then will I hear from heaven, and will forgive their sin, and will heal their land.* 2 Chronicles 7:14

However, God is just as realistic as He is hopeful. Though God would rather resurrect relationships, He recognizes resurrection is not going to occur in every situation. God knows that due to different reasons (the hardness of our hearts, the unwillingness of our spouse and our emotional capacity to withstand a particular circumstance) that divorce is, in certain cases, unavoidable. And so God has made provisions to allow His children to break the marriage covenant.

Seven Common Excuses for Divorce

1. Oops, I made a stupid mistake.

2. The pressure is just too great.

3. Our sexual relationship is no longer meeting my needs.

4. We are no longer in love, so it would be a shame to continue in the relationship. We need to be honest with our true feelings.

5. He/she is not the person I married. I could not have anticipated his/her change of character.

6. He/she is, unfortunately, still the person I married. I thought I could change my spouse, but I was wrong.

7. We seem to have irreconcilable differences. We have to divorce.

If you divorce for any of these reasons, you are outside the will of God. Your divorce is invalid, and your spiritual union is still intact. This means you are neither spiritually free to remarry nor free from your divine bond to your mate. Sure, the judge said you were single, but God says you are still under the covenant.

None of these EXCUSES are valid. Here are the only three biblically valid reasons for divorce:

THE ONLY VALID REASONS FOR DIVORCE ARE:

Adultery

Abandonment

Physical Abuse

Reason 1 - Adultery

We live in a society that not only mocks God and His church but also mocks righteousness and holiness. In an atmosphere such as this, it is no wonder infidelity is regarded by many as no big deal. Husbands cheat on wives, wives cheat on husbands, and they act as though it is one big game. TV shows, movies, music and pop culture as a whole glorify the culture of infidelity.

And when the church attempts to raise a finger in protest, society is quick to point out the skeletons in the closet of the church and its servants. Publicized instances of ministers and pastors caught cheating have created a climate wherein people will often say, "If cheating is so wrong, why are so many church folks doing it?" This is a foolish argument.

First of all, while it may be true some pastors have fallen prey to the spirit of adultery, there are still scores of us who refuse to fall prey to adultery. We remain faithful to our spouses and faithful to God. Secondly, man's hypocrisy does not void God's Word.

God could not be any clearer about his disgust with adultery. Even a child in Sunday school who has learned the Ten Commandments knows,

Thou shalt not commit adultery.

Exodus 20:14

It should be clear then not only is adultery a big deal, but adultery is a major violation of God's law. It is a reprehensible behavior undermining the sanctity of the marriage union by causing a separation in the spiritual connectivity uniting husband and wife. Therefore, the person who has suffered this offense has the biblical justification for formalizing the separation through a divorce. They are free to end the marriage. By doing so, they will not be in sin, and the community of believers should accept them without judgment or rebuke. They are free to get remarried after the divorce has been finalized.

Don't rush into another relationship right away, though. There should be a period of time set aside for the purpose of healing and recovery. As a pastor and counselor, I know the very worst thing someone can do after being devastated by infidelity and divorce is to immediately start dating someone else. You will not be ready. Before you love again, God needs to heal the open wounds in your heart and soul. This takes time. How long? It depends on the individual. There is no set time. But I do know a week, a month, even six months is too soon to think about getting serious with someone else after a divorce.

Another reason you want to take it slow is that you need time to reflect on what went wrong. Since you don't want to keep making the same mistake over and over again, it would behoove you to prayerfully figure out the part you may have played in your marriage's demise. I know it wasn't your fault. Your cheating spouse was the one who is to blame. This may be true. But, it is also true, in almost every case I encounter, both parties could have done more to affair-proof their marriage.

While nothing justifies cheating, there are things husbands and wives could have done to prevent it. For instance, the long-term and willful withholding of physical or emotional intimacy can create a condition where infidelity is more likely to occur. A spouse, who physically or emotionally ignores their mate, will open the door for someone else to come in and seduce them with attention and kindness. It's not right, but it's a reality. If couples do not maintain emotional intimacy, then it leaves them open to the possibility of satisfying their needs through outside means. Consequently, after your divorce, examine yourself and ask yourself; did I practice the five rules for a healthy and affair-proof marriage?

Five Rules for a Healthy and Affair-Proof Marriage

Be thankful for your spouse

Practice communicating from the heart

Be intimate

Practice the power of forgiveness

Be teachable

After examining yourself, you may come to the conclusion you did indeed do all you could to establish a healthy union. You practiced the aforementioned rules. You tried to make it work. And yet, your spouse was determined to take advantage of you and violate the covenant. If this is the case, you still need to take it slow and let God confirm this reality in your spirit. By confirming it to you, He will release you from doubts and destructive self-questioning. This process takes time.

The main point here is infidelity authorizes you to end your marriage. Of course, you are not obligated to end your marriage; you can also choose to stay with your spouse after they have been caught cheating. Couples who stay together after infidelity need to make church and pastoral counseling their top priority. Also, the person who cheated must want to change and must agree to stop all contact with the other man/woman. This means no phone calls, no email, no text messages, no Facebook, and no so-called chance meetings in the supermarket. There must be a complete and total break.

The person who makes a decision to forgive and stay will eventually need to let go of the past and embrace the future. You will never forget what happened to you, but by staying with your spouse, you are committing yourself not to let the past be a constant stumbling block to your future happiness. Once your spouse has demonstrated they have changed their ways and are ready to regain your trust, you don't have the right to bring up past offenses and throw them in their face every time you get angry.

You cannot bring up the affair just because you're mad, because the grass isn't cut, or the laundry isn't washed. If you decide to stay and work it out, and it truly does get worked out, then you have lost your ability to go back into the past and reopen a closed case. You cannot divorce your husband today over an affair that took place twenty years ago. If you wanted a divorce, you should have done so then instead of deciding to stay.

Not everyone has the strength to stay and forgive. If not, that's OK. It's far better to make a clean break than to continue in a situation doomed to failure. If you know the memories of infidelity will continue to haunt you and replay in your mind, then God allows you to end the union and sever the spiritual ties.

Reason 2 – Abandonment

Remember the saying *it takes two to tango*. Well, it also takes two to be married. You can graduate in absentia, be convicted of criminal charges in absentia and vote in absentia, but you cannot be married in absentia. In order for the marriage to work in the way God intended, the husband and wife need to live together as one. Husband and wife must live under the same roof. They should sleep in the same bed. There should be mutual participation in each other's lives.

When two people are married, then singular pronouns like mine and yours become plural pronouns like us and ours, as in our bank account, our home, our children, and our future. This shared existence is what God intended when He declared in Genesis 2: 18: *[It is] not good that the man should be alone…*

When a husband or a wife leaves their spouse alone or abandoned, then they have breached the marriage contract. The Apostle Paul addresses this issue in his letter to the Corinthians.

Paul wrote in 1 Corinthians 7:13-16:

> *To the rest I say this (I, not the Lord): If any brother has a wife who is not a believer and she is willing to live with him, he must not divorce her. And if a woman has a husband who is not a believer and he is willing to live with her, she must not divorce him. For the unbelieving husband has been sanctified through his wife, and the unbelieving wife has been sanctified through her believing husband. Otherwise your children would be unclean, but as it is, they are holy. But if the unbeliever leaves, let him do so. A believing man or woman is not bound in such circumstances; God has called us to live in peace. How do you know, wife, whether you will save your husband? Or, how do you know, husband, whether you will save your wife?*

Based on the doctrine outlined in this verse, we know the voluntary departure of one spouse gives the other a spiritually valid reason to divorce. This teaching reflects the reality that no one can be married all by themselves. Therefore, when a husband or wife separates from the physical proximity of their spouse, they have violated the cohabitation rule God wove into the fabric of marriage. Without cohabitation, the husband and wife are estranged. Permanent estrangement makes it impossible for a godly marriage to continue.

How can you plan a future if you have no idea when or if your mate will ever return? It is impossible to drink out of the marriage cup with someone who isn't there. Moreover, abandonment suggests your spouse has left you to start a whole new life without you. Hence, there is an understanding they have no intentions of ever living in covenant with you again.

Please note, however, if you throw your spouse out or force them to leave, that is not abandonment; you cannot kick your husband out of the house, change the locks, and then cry out, "He abandoned me! He abandoned me!" It doesn't work like that.

Also, a spouse who stays out all night or doesn't come home on the weekends hasn't abandoned you. This behavior is sinful and wrong, but it cannot be classified as abandonment. Nor is abandonment the justifiable separation that can sometimes force couples apart. These unavoidable instances of temporary separation include:

Military Service

Temporary Job Transfers

Hospitalizations

For the sake of further clarity, consider Webster's definition of abandonment: a·ban·don (verb): to leave completely and finally; forsake utterly; desert.

The doctrine Paul articulates makes it clear that, in the case of abandonment, divorce is an acceptable response. There is no cause for shame. There is no need for you to repent. By divorcing your absentee spouse, you are merely finalizing their cowardly decision and bringing closure to an indefinite separation. After the divorce, you are free to heal and move on with your life without being spiritually tied to your departed ex.

Reason 3 - Physical Abuse

Wives are partners; they are not punching bags. When a man is covered in a demonic spirit of violence, then the faith that God placed in the marriage union is broken. Here's the proof:

> *I hate a man's covering himself with violence as well as with his garment, says the LORD Almighty. So guard yourself in your spirit, and do not break faith. Malachi 2:16*

Violence breaks the faith because faith cannot dwell amidst terror and intimidation. The husband, who has been entrusted by God to protect his wife but then becomes her attacker, has broken his faith commitment as her husband. In fact, he has relinquished his role altogether. God stipulates a husband is one who guards his wife; therefore, a man who beats his wife is not a husband. He is a thug, a tormentor, a criminal.

Although verbal and emotional abuses are wrong, physical abuse is even worse; it is a justification for divorce. As previously stated, any man who breaks the faith by covering himself with violence isn't worthy of being a husband.

A wife who has been physically harmed by her husband has a legitimate reason to leave and never look back. God never intended for women to suffer physical abuse and torment at the hands of the one person in the world who is supposed to love them, as Christ loves the church. He doesn't expect you to jeopardize your life in the name of submitting to someone who cannot be trusted to keep you safe.

Anyone who has ever counseled abused women will attest to the fact that getting out of abusive situations is never easy. There are serious financial, social and logistical barriers keeping many women bound in abusive homes. This is an unfortunate reality.

Nonetheless, despite the fear and hesitation, if your life is in jeopardy, you must take action to preserve yourself. There are churches, shelters and ministries that can stand in the gap and assist you to safety. Most importantly, though, if you believe God is truly all-powerful and almighty, you'll have to rely on Him to help you make it through and send people whom you can trust your way. Pray about it. Ask God to give you a plan, give you the means, and make a way of escape for you and your children. Here are a few trusted, safe and confidential resources to help you.

National Domestic Violence Hotline
1-800-799-7233 (1-800-799-SAFE)

TTY: 1-800-787-3224

Institute on Domestic Violence in the African-American Community
www.dvinstitute.org

Life Source Consultants Inc.
314-524-0686

contact@lifesourceconsultants.org

While the latter part of this chapter dealt with breaking the commitment, you will recall the bulk of the chapter was a call toward commitment. By titling this chapter, *Commitment in the Cup*, I am keeping the focus on preserving marriage as opposed to dissolving marriage. In narrowing the marriage escape clause to three specific biblically valid reasons, I discount the multitude of invalid excuses people use, which results in unauthorized divorces. Therefore, my goal has been to illustrate the commitment in the marriage cup is strong and not easily broken.

Christian couples must embrace this truth. We have to see marriage as the life-long union it was created to be. This knowledge will transform your behavior. It will give you the power to hang in there during the ups and downs of your relationship. Whenever the devil tries to tempt you into throwing in the towel and walking away: rebuke him. Plead the Blood of Jesus. Remind yourself that God put the commitment in the cup.

Chapter Three

Intimacy in the Cup

Marriage is more than just an institution. Marriage is a privilege. Marriage is a blessing. Marriage is an arrangement that satisfies a man's natural desires. We know this because of the story of Adam in the garden. The Bible doesn't give us all the details of creation, but we do know one day, God saw Adam's need and decided to bless him.

I can imagine on that day, the voice of the Lord walked through the garden and appeared unto Adam, "Adam, since you have pleased me in the spiritual, now I am going to create an arrangement to please you in the natural. I want you to experience natural love and affection in the same way your worship and service to me have given you spiritual love and affection. Finally, Adam, since you have achieved spiritual wholeness, you're now ready for natural wholeness."

You see, a whole person in covenant with another whole person is the formula for natural wholeness. And so God created Eve and the institution of marriage to give Adam and the rest of us natural intimacy. In other words, marriage was created to be a conduit for closeness, love and intimacy.

So what happens if these benefits are absent from your marriage cup? What happens if your marriage is not producing the fruit of closeness, affection and intimacy? If your marriage is not acting as a conduit for natural intimacy, then God's primary reason for bringing you a wife or a husband has been undermined. In other words, when you are married, but do not enjoy emotional, physical and natural intimacy, then you might as well be single. This is what the Devil wants.

Since the beginning of time, the Devil has been going into homes, trying to drive a wedge between husband and wife. One of the Devil's greatest tricks in his campaign to destroy marriage has been to convince couples to pour intimacy out of the marriage cup. The Devil has convinced far too many married couples it's normal for passion, affection and intimacy to die as the marriage progresses past the newlywed phase. As a result of this deception, many married couples stand by and do nothing as all the intimacy slowly leaks out of their marriage cup. What a terrible mistake. The Devil does not want you to know maintaining intimacy is crucial to maintaining a happy and healthy marriage.

Without intimacy, marriage disintegrates into a dry, stale arrangement, as opposed to the fulfilling partnership it was created to be. Once we let our marriage become dry, it is no wonder we begin to get bored with our spouse and get tempted by the lure of the exciting, mysterious stranger.

Moreover, the loss of intimacy in marriage means some husbands think it's normal not to be attracted to their wives. Similarly, some wives think it is ok if their most personal conversations take place with people other than their husbands. These problems are to be expected whenever there is an intimacy leak in your marriage cup. Intimacy is the substance that keeps a marriage fresh and satisfying. Intimacy produces closeness. Intimacy is the difference between loving and being in love.

THE SIGNS OF AN INTIMACY LEAK

Spending less free time together

No kissing, hugging or very little physical contact

You have stopped making each other laugh and do not
have fun together

You sleep in separate beds

Constant arguing and insults

Lack of concern for one another

Lack of respect

As you read the signs, you may come to the realization, "Yes, I could use some more intimacy in my marriage cup." There is no shame in this realization. All is not lost. In fact, recognizing there is an intimacy shortage, though upsetting, is a lot better than ignoring the problem or, worse, being dishonest with yourself.

In all forms of recovery, the first step in fixing the problem is admitting that there is a problem. Once you have acknowledged the leak, you can begin to take the necessary steps to regain lost intimacy and bring your marriage back into God's divine order. The remainder of this chapter will be devoted to outlining three ways to maintain intimacy in the marriage relationship.

Step One

Maintaining Intimacy

Be Equally Yoked

The first and most important step in ushering intimacy into your marriage is to make sure you are equally yoked in a divine spiritual covenant. Being equally yoked in a spiritual covenant means you and your spouse are committed Christians brought together by God and held together by a spiritual bond, which no man can put asunder. Living under the authority of this kind of covenant enables you to experience true intimacy. In fact, if you do not have a spiritually covenanted marriage, then you will never achieve the soothing, soul-satisfying intimacy God wants you to have.

The reason is this; the only vine upon which the fruit of intimacy can grow is the spiritual vine. Or, to put it another way, true intimacy can only develop when two people are spiritually in sync and spiritually bonded to one another. Now, I know this stands in contradiction to what you may hear on TV talk shows and in the media.

The world teaches affection, shared goals, common background and natural compatibility to create intimacy. There is even an internet dating website promising people intimacy through compatibility testing. But being compatible does not guarantee intimacy. There are scores of couples who are compatible but lack intimacy. Even more surprising is the fact that love does not guarantee intimacy. There are scores of husbands who sincerely love their wives but share no intimacy with them. Intimacy requires more than compatibility. Intimacy requires more than love. Intimacy requires a spiritual bond.

When a husband is spiritually connected to his wife, and vice versa, they will share a level of intimacy that love, by itself, can never produce. Think of it this way; God loves the world, and He loves sinners. But God is not intimate with the world. He is not intimate with sinners. The only people with whom God is intimate are those to whom he is spiritually connected through His Holy Spirit.

In this same vein, a husband must do more than love his wife if he wants to share intimacy with her. In order to achieve intimacy, he must be spiritually connected to her. This is why having a spiritually covenanted marriage is the most important step you can take in satisfying your natural need for intimacy.

But for the sake of clarity, let's explore the three alternatives to the spiritual covenant. These covenants make the release of true intimacy impossible. They are:

The Counterfeit Covenant
The Partial Covenant
The Compromised Covenant

Counterfeit Covenant: This is the union of two unbelievers whose marriage has not been sanctioned by God and who live outside the rules and authority of God.

A couple (in some jurisdictions, even a same-sex couple) can enter into a legally valid marriage by simply obtaining a marriage license, paying the necessary fees and taxes and standing before a judge or minister to exchange vows. Once these stipulations are met, the state will issue the couple a marriage certificate certifying their union is legitimate. But just because a marriage is valid in the eyes of the state doesn't mean it's valid in God's eyes. In God's eyes, the marriage covenant between two unbelievers isn't valid - it's counterfeit.

The unbelievers' marriage covenant is counterfeit because the Holy Spirit isn't present to seal the union. Without the Holy Spirit joining husband and wife together, instead of closeness, there is spiritual separation. Separation at the spiritual level rules out any hope of obtaining intimacy.

Those who enter into a counterfeit covenant are trying to obtain that which is unattainable to them. The most anyone living in a counterfeit covenant can hope to have is counterfeit intimacy. When confronted with this reality, unbelievers can either live in frustration, live in sadness, or live in denial. But, even in denial, there will always be a still, small voice within them, reminding them that there is emptiness where intimacy should be.

Partial Covenant: The union of a believer and an unbeliever. While the believer is subject to the rules governing marriage and divorce, the unbeliever is not. Therefore, only half of the union is under covenantal authority.

There are two ways a partial covenant can be established:

1. **A believer willfully and knowingly marries an unbeliever.**

2. **During the course of a marriage between two unbelievers, one person accepts Christ, and their spouse does not.**

In a partially covenanted marriage, the believing spouse is spiritually bound to the unbelieving spouse, but the unbelieving spouse is not spiritually bound to the believing spouse. Why? Because unbelievers have neither the Holy Spirit nor a relationship of accountability with Jesus Christ. Remember, no one can serve two masters, and the master you serve determines the rules by which you must live. If Jesus is your master, He requires you to be bound to your mate. However, if Satan is your master, he wants you bound only to sin.

So, in a partial covenant, spiritual connectivity only flows in one direction. As a result, intimacy can only flow in one direction. The believer can offer intimacy to the unbeliever, but the unbeliever, lacking a spiritual connection, cannot reciprocate.

The most that can be attained in a partial covenant is partial intimacy, and partial intimacy is just about as useful as a house with a partial roof. I suppose it is better than a house with no roof at all, but it is far from ideal.

Compromised Covenant: A covenant between two believers wherein one or both of them refuse to live up to their spiritually mandated roles.

In a compromised covenant, a spiritual connection exists, but all the blessings that should go along with being connected have been blocked. Disobedience, rebellion, or too much sin in the matrimonial camp has caused a rift in the flow of closeness and intimacy. Instead of being each other's best friend, husband and wife become adversarial towards one another. Although they are still spiritually bound, sin has driven them emotionally apart. The situation becomes more dire as the promise of the spiritual covenant becomes more compromised. Instead of getting better, the couple gets bitter.

The fallacies in the preceding covenant models bring me back to my original assertion; the first order of business is attaining the intimacy your marriage needs and your desire to do everything in your power to become equally yoked in a healthy and stable spiritual covenant.

This means if you and your spouse are in a counterfeit covenant, then let God become the Lord of your lives. Turn off Dr. Phil. Turn off Oprah. They can't give you what you need; only God can give you what you need. God is the only one who has the power to save your soul, save your life, and save your marriage.

Once you and your partner give God your lives, He will teach you His ways. The Bible says Christ came to give us not only life but more abundant life. The implication here is until you are connected with God, you don't have the fullness of anything. Apart from God, you don't know what love is. You don't know what closeness is. You don't know what intimacy is. You think you know, but how can you? In order to know how to be intimate with another person, you must first learn how to be intimate with God. As you and your partner move closer to God, you will move closer to one another. Then, intimacy will finally flow through your union.

If you are a believer in a partially covenanted marriage, then God wants you to be a catalyst for change. As the believing spouse, your mission is to let your light shine so brightly that your partner gets tired of the darkness and wants to be equally yoked with you in the faith. It may take a while for this to happen. But, no matter how long it takes, don't get discouraged and don't let your spouse's stubbornness cause you to doubt your power to lead them into change. Paul wrote in 1 Corinthians 7:14:

> *For the unbelieving husband is sanctified by the wife, and the unbelieving wife is sanctified by the husband: else were your children unclean; but now are they holy.*

The hope Paul gave unequally yoked Corinthian couples is also available for you. So, when the Devil tries to convince you to give up on your unbelieving spouse, tell the Devil to get lost. When the enemy tries to convince you that you are destined to live in a permanent state of intimacy deprivation because your spouse will never be able to give you the closeness you crave, tell the Devil to get behind you. Remind yourself, "He that is within me is stronger than he that is within the world." 1 John 14:4

Moreover, instead of constantly complaining about your situation, instead of always going to the Pastor crying about how lonely you are, make up your mind to change your circumstance. You can change your circumstance by tapping into the power of the blood. Ask God to help you sanctify your spouse through your own commitment. If you stay steadfast in this mission, then one day, you will reap your reward when your partial intimacy becomes whole.

And finally, for those living in compromised covenants, the only way you will ever recover your intimacy is to bring yourself into proper spiritual alignment with God. Repent of your sins. Turn away from rebellion and disobedience, so the blessings can flow again. If you have sinned against your wife, ask for her forgiveness and recommit yourself to your marriage. If you sinned against your husband, tell him how sorry you are and how your mind is determined to become the wife he needs. If you have sinned against each other, call a family meeting where you recommit the household back to God. Pray together. Fast together. Pray for each other. Do whatever it takes and give up whatever it takes to bring the intimacy back into the cup. The point I have tried to convey in this section is, as the Bible says, God is the source from which all good things flow. Since intimacy is a good thing, to acquire it, you must start with spirituality.

However, if you want to keep intimacy, you can't just stay in the spiritual; you must also work in the natural. Faith without works is dead. In order to maintain intimacy, even after you have made sure you are equally yoked in a spiritual covenant, your work isn't over. Beyond your spiritual commitment, you must also be committed to doing the natural activities God has ordained as intimacy-producing.

The two natural activities God placed in the marriage cup for their intimacy-producing power are sex and romance. And as you will see, under the umbrella of romance are communication, fellowship, thoughtfulness and cooperation. Let's start by turning our attention to the discussion of sex.

Step Two

Maintain Physical Attraction

and a Healthy Sex Life

It never ceases to amaze me that whenever I discuss sex from the pulpit, married couples seem to get uncomfortable. It's as though some people believe pastoral instruction should be limited to topics such as faith and prayer. Unfortunately, some people are determined to spiritualize the natural. Don't let spooky spirituality hijack your understanding of the role of sex.

Face it, sex is, and will always be, an important fact of life. If you doubt this assertion, just turn on the TV or open a magazine. Every other ad will be about sex, or so it will seem. There are pharmaceutical ads promising to fix sexual disorders; there are dating sites hinting at the allure of sex; and there are, of course, a host of ads using sex to sell everything from blue jeans to sports cars.

While Madison Avenue uses sex to sell, God gave sex to married couples to solidify and strengthen the covenant. Outside the confines of marriage, sex is not only dangerous; it's immoral, sinful and socially destructive. I want every single person to know that fornication is wrong. But, once a man and a woman unite in holy matrimony, then they are free to reap all of the intimacy-building benefits that sex brings. Not only are married couples free to reap the benefits of sex, but if husband and wife are physically able, God wants them to have sex. God desires married folks to have not just any sex but good and passionate sex.

Read the following scriptures to see the mind of God concerning these issues:

1 Corinthians 7:3-5

[3]The husband should fulfill his marital duty to his wife, and likewise the wife to her husband. [4]The wife's body does not belong to her alone but also to her husband. In the same way, the husband's body does not belong to him alone but also to his wife. [5]Do not deprive each other except by mutual consent and for a time, so that you may devote yourselves to prayer. Then come together again so that Satan will not tempt you because of your lack of self-control.

Proverbs 5:18-20

[18]May your fountain be blessed, and may you rejoice in the wife of your youth. [19]A loving doe, a graceful deer - may her breasts satisfy you always, may you ever be captivated by her love. [20]Why be captivated, my son by an adulteress? Why embrace the bosom of another man's wife?

Song of Songs 5:10-16

[10][Beloved] my lover is radiant and ruddy, outstanding among ten thousand. [11]His head is purest gold; his hair is wavy and black as a raven. [12]His eyes are like doves by the water streams, washed in milk, mounted like jewels. [13]His cheeks are like beds of spice yielding perfume. His lips are like lilies dripping with myrrh. [14]His arms are rods of gold set with chrysolite. His body is like polished ivory

decorated with sapphires. [15] His legs are pillars of marble set on bases of pure gold. His appearance is like Lebanon, choice as its cedars. [16] His mouth is sweetness itself; he is altogether lovely. This is my lover, this is my friend ...

A careful consideration of these scriptures reveals God has placed certain blessings in sex that should be drained and poured into the marriage cup. Sex, done in the atmosphere of a committed, monogamous marriage, yields intimacy and closeness. Unselfish and mutually satisfying sex brings couples into spiritual closeness with one another. That's right, the physical act of sex is also a spiritual act.

When a husband physically bonds with his wife, they affirm their oneness and their spiritual union. Therefore, it is difficult for couples who have healthy portions of sex and romance to drift apart emotionally. Sure, drifting apart can still happen, but the likelihood of sexually healthy couples drifting apart is far less than couples who don't have good and frequent sex.

A NOTE ABOUT PHYSICAL ATTRACTION AND SEX

Foreplay is not just the physical activity you engage in before sex, but foreplay is the act of creating an environment where sex is desirable. Getting your hair done, keeping your body neat and clean and making sure you are physically desirable to your mate are all forms of foreplay. Neither a man nor a woman is going to be excited about having sex with someone to whom he/she is not physically attracted. Sex involves physical stimulation and attraction. You don't have sex with someone's mind or with their personality; you have sex with their body. So becoming the kind of eye candy your partner likes is foreplay. Don't let anyone tell you that keeping the passion flames burning is unimportant. Seduction is good for your sex life, and it's good for your marriage.

Step Three

Create Romance

When I counsel couples, I usually spend the first part of the counseling session trying to determine their strengths and weaknesses in their marriage. Most of the time, this leads me to ask the couple to describe the level of intimacy in their marriage.

Let's explore the fictional life of Jack and Jill. Jack and Jill have come to pastoral counseling because Jill feels there's something missing from their marriage.

> **Pastor:** *So, how would you two rate the level of intimacy in your marriage?*

> Jack responds, smiling, obviously very proud of himself.

> **Jack:** *Great! The Mrs. and I have sex all the time ... and not just sex ... we have great sex. So I guess I would have to give us a ten.*

> **Pastor:** *Ok, that's good. Now, let me hear from your wife. Jill, how would you rate the intimacy in your marriage?*

> **Jill:** *I suppose it's pretty good. I mean, I really do love my husband, and he works really hard.*

> **Pastor:** *Well, I'm glad to hear he works hard, but I'm asking you about intimacy. How is the intimacy?*

> **Jill:** *Like I said, Pastor, I would say it's pretty good.*

At this point, Jack, who has been sitting back with his chest stuck out, begins to lose a bit of his grin and sits up.

>*Jack: Go ahead, Jill, tell the man ... our sex life is great. I mean, I haven't ever heard you complain about how I handle my business in the bedroom, right?*

Clearing his throat, the pastor looks at Jack.

>*Pastor: Thanks, Jack, but I want Jill to tell me in her own words. Go ahead, Jill.*

>*Jill: Well, Pastor, Jack is right; he is a wonderful lover, and he does satisfy me.*

The smile creeps back on Jack's face.

>*Pastor: OK. But ...?*

>*Jill: Maybe I'm just being silly or unrealistic. You know I always did like those romantic fairy tales. It's just that sometimes I want to be intimate with my husband without going upstairs to the bedroom. You know, sometimes I just want to hold his hand; sometimes I just want him to hold me. Sometimes I just want to hear him tell me how much he loves me.*

>*Now, don't get me wrong, it's not that I don't like sex, but sometimes, I just want to be held.*

Pausing for a moment, she asks, *"Does that seem strange?"*

Glancing over at Jack, I can tell he is at a complete loss for words.

> **Pastor:** *No, Jill, that doesn't sound odd at all. And by the way, Jack, don't feel bad. I want both of you to listen to what I am about to say because your experience is quite common. The problem is while sex is important for creating intimacy, there is more to intimacy than just sex. Most men, and even some women, have forgotten that romance is different from sex. Romance is an important part of intimacy. The kissing, the hugging, the sweet words and the tender looks, all of these love transactions are intimacy-producing activities. I want you to have strong and lasting intimacy, and I especially want you to hear this, Jack; you can't just master lovemaking, but you've got to master romance-making as well. Do you see what I mean?*

> **Jack:** *I don't know if I do... this whole romance thing just isn't me.*

> **Pastor:** *Well, take a few weeks to think about it. We'll talk later.*

{To be continued}

I share this story because it illustrates a poignant truth: if you are serious about keeping intimacy in your marriage cup, then you must develop intimacy outside of the bedroom. This is especially true given the reality that sex will not always be an option for married couples. There are couples who, because of serious medical reasons, cannot engage in sexual intercourse. Disease, injury, impotency, physical condition, as well as a woman's monthly menstrual cycle will prevent couples from engaging in sex. Also, beyond medical reasons, there is a host of other reasons that may cause a sex drought in the marriage.

I often advise singles they should never rush down the aisle just to have sex. If sex is the only thing motivating you to want to get married, then you are going to be sorely disappointed once you're hit with the reality of married life. I tell them, contrary to what you are hoping, no married couple can spend all day in bed satisfying each other's flesh.

Married life is demanding and full of responsibilities, obligations, and commitments. When you're married, bills must be paid, children must be raised, and the home must be managed. These activities will encroach upon sex time.

When you have a crying baby in one room, a basket full of dirty clothes in the other room and dinner in the oven, then even a quickie is too much to manage. Therefore, couples need to have enough romance in their marriage to sustain their intimacy through the business of life. Take note, men, even when you can't make love, you ought to be making romance.

Back to the story of Jack and Jill:

> **Pastor:** *So, Jack and Jill, now it's been a few weeks since our last conversation; how's the intimacy been?*

> **Jack:** *Well, Pastor, let me put it this way; since Jill and I have been married, I have always taken pride in the fact I was a good husband. I support my wife and love her dearly.*

> *Up until a few months ago, I figured Jill was about as happy as a wife could be. I took care of her financial and physical needs, so last time*

when you asked us about our intimacy, I just knew my wife was going to start telling you about how great I am... I know, Pastor, don't laugh.

Anyway, when she started to open up and confessed there were some needs I wasn't taking care of, I was hurt. In fact, I went home hurt and upset. I think it took a day or two before I said more than a few words to her. But then, one night, I was lying in bed, wide awake; and I could tell she was awake too. The kids were fast asleep, and I could hear the rain hitting the bedroom window. Now, the old me would have rolled over and started trying to get busy, if you know what I mean. But then I remembered the look on my wife's face that day in your office when she was talking about her feelings. I hate to see my wife troubled. So here's what I did, I switched on the radio and turned on some nice, soft jazz. I got up out of bed and went over to my wife. I took her by the hand; then, guess what I did?

Pastor: *What did you do?*

Jack: *I led her out of bed, put her head on my shoulder, and right there in the middle of the night, with the sound of rain and jazz playing in the background, I began to dance with my wife.*

We danced, and I held her close. After a few songs, we lay back down on the bed and talked. We talked about everything, and we talked about nothing. I made her laugh as we reminisced about our honeymoon. Since we didn't have much money, we ended up staying in this motel that was so rundown we had to sleep in our clothes.

As we talked, every now and then, she would lean up and kiss me on my lips. Then, we kept right on talking. Before we realized it, the sun was up. We spent all night holding each other and laughing. And you know what, Pastor?

Pastor: *What?*

Jack: *I have never felt more intimacy between us than I did that night. It's like a light bulb went off in my head. I finally understood what my wife was talking about. I felt so close to her. I felt like I did back when we were dating. Listen to this; the next day at work, I called her on my lunch break. I was all baby this and sweetheart that. It wasn't like I was trying to be romantic, but after the night before, it just started coming out. I didn't know I had it in me. I guess all I'm trying to say is, thank you. Thank you for teaching me something I would never have figured out on my own. I just hate that I let all this time pass without knowing what real romance was.*

Pastor: *Jack, that's great news. I'm glad to hear it. What about you, Jill? What's your take?*

Jill: *Pastor, I've been sitting here fighting back the tears. I am so grateful. I am grateful to you for taking the time to help my husband and me. I am grateful to my husband for making me the happiest woman on earth; these past few months have been better than any fairy tale I have ever read. But, most of all, I am grateful to God. I am grateful to Him for blessing me with a husband. God is so wonderful. I know what you mean when you tell us marriage is a privilege and a blessing.*

My natural self feels satisfied and fulfilled. The intimacy my marriage has brought me only makes me want to worship God more.

Pastor: *You both have blessed me with your testimony. Now, you know what you've got to do, don't you?*

Jack and Jill: *What's that, Pastor?*

Pastor: *You've got to share this testimony with your friends, especially you, Jack. If your buddies come to you talking about what a hassle it is to be married, I want you to tell them about what you learned. Tell them the same God who helped fix your marriage can do the same for them. Since everybody is not going to come in here and talk to the pastor, I am counting on people like you to take the truth to them.*

Jack: *You know, I think I can do that. I bet if enough men take the lead, our church is going to be filled with blessed marriages.*

Pastor: *You're right. That would be a blessing.*

Jack and Jill's success was based on the realization that good marriages take work. Good marriages are not accidents, and luck plays no role. When you see a couple enjoying one another and living in marital bliss, then you know they have worked long and hard to get to that point.

When the football game was on, that husband (at least, every now and then) made a conscious decision to turn off the game and go romance his wife by taking her for a long walk in the park. Similarly, that wife, instead of going out with the girls every weekend, committed herself to make sure some weekends, she tells the girls no and her husband yes.

This is what it takes to make romance. It takes sacrifice. It takes time. It takes communication and commitment. When romance is achieved, the marriage cup gets sweeter and more refreshing. So, don't let the flames die out. Pursue passionate romance with your spouse, and rekindle the fire that drew you together.

Chapter Four
Authority and Order
in the Cup

Once upon a time, words like submission, deference, obedience and authority used to resonate within us. We proudly included these words in our wedding vows, sermons and everyday vernacular. Times have changed. The devil has worked hard to make these words, and more importantly, the ideas they represent, a source of anger, animosity and indignation. The enemy has made it so that when you use these words, you do so at your own peril. Whether you are a parent speaking to a child, a boss speaking to an employee or a coach talking to a star athlete, when you speak of authority, brace yourself.

Making an appeal to authority threatens the status quo and challenges strongly held beliefs. The most potent is the belief that accepting authority is tantamount to denying individual rights and personal freedom.

The so-called liberated man and liberated woman have convinced themselves no one has the right to control their behavior or place limitations on the exercise of their will. Furthermore, they live under the belief they have the right to do whatever they want to do, whenever they want to do it. Their attitudes and dispositions reveal they hate authority.

Anyone who hates authority is ignorant of two very important truths:

1. **Authority comes from God.**
2. **Authority works to protect you.**

As difficult as it may sometimes be to submit to authority, try to imagine what the world would be like if there were no systems of authority in place to protect us. Think about how confusing and chaotic the roads and highways would be without stop signs, traffic lights or speed limits. It would be a nightmare. Without the authority of the stop sign, there would be nothing to prevent a speeding truck from smashing into your car at an intersection.

Fortunately, there is an authority on the roadways. We can take comfort in the fact there are rules governing what the car next to us can and cannot do. And we can feel relatively safe because we know the authorities, a.k.a. police officers and highway patrolmen, are there to ensure people obey the rules.

Now, this is what baffles me: if people are wise enough to know we need an authority on the roadways, then shouldn't everyone also agree we need authority in our homes and marriages as well? Of course, we should. Just as the authority on the roadways keeps us safe, authority in the home also keeps us safe.

When a wife submits to the authority of a godly husband, and a godly husband submits himself to the authority of Christ, then both husband and wife are covered under divine protection. A wife, who knows she is under the authority of a godly leader, knows she is protected from abandonment and helplessness. She knows since she lives under the covering of her husband, she also lives in the care of her husband.

Likewise, a husband, who has submitted himself to Christ, knows he doesn't have to bear the burden of headship on his own because Christ is there to strengthen him in his leadership role. Therefore, keep in mind, submitting to authority works for you and not against you.

But, if authority is going to be fully present in your marriage cup, then there must be accountability. Accountability signifies both husband and wife know they have different roles, and they know they are answerable to one another in regard to the fulfillment of their roles.

Don't let the fact that husbands and wives have unique and separate duties be a stumbling block for you. Man and woman united by a spiritual covenant are definitely one, yet they are not the same; oneness does not equal sameness. Be advised there are certain functions only a husband can fulfill and certain functions only a wife can fulfill. The idea men and women are the same and can live in a same-role marriage is almost as bad as the idea of same-sex marriage. Common sense dictates if God wanted us to be the same, then He wouldn't have made us different. Celebrating and recognizing the inherent differences between the sexes is one of the keys to a happy marriage.

Science provides a wonderful example of this principle. Think about how magnets bond to one another. Two magnets whose poles are the same will never bond to each other. In fact, they will repel one another. The stronger you try to push them together, the harder they will push away from each other. However, when you take away the sameness and make the poles different, negative to positive and positive to negative, then the two magnets are capable of creating a bond so strong, so tight, and so close no man can pull them apart. This is where we get the expression, opposites attract. The strength of the attraction is only made possible by honoring inherent differences.

So as you read the following sections, keep in mind the duties of a husband are supposed to be fundamentally different from the duties of a wife. When God created man and woman, He intentionally gave us separate identities and functions. Now, this assertion may not fall in line with political correctness or feminist ideals, but the Word of God was never meant to be acceptable to man's philosophies and wisdom. Remember, the wisdom of God is foolishness to man; therefore, you have a choice: do you want your marriage to be right in God's eyes or man's eyes?

In order for your marriage to be blessed by God, you have to accept there is strength in difference, strength in authority and strength in order. Now with these truths in mind, let's consider the duties of a wife and the duties of a husband.

The Duties of a Wife

Be a Benefit

For the man is not of the woman, · but the woman of the man. Neither was the man created for the woman; but the woman for the man.
1 Corinthians 11:8-9

And the LORD God said, [It is] not good that the man should be alone; I will make him a help meet for him. *Genesis 2: 18*

These verses make it clear that one of the most important duties of a wife is to be a helpmate or a benefit to her husband.

Being a benefit is not a demeaning role; it is a role of honor and glory. A benefit can make a tedious life a happy life. For example, there are certain jobs no one would dare take if it were not for the benefits. Soldiers who volunteer for military service and who are sent to war zones know they are going to receive a financial benefit for every day they spend in harm's way. Hazardous duty pay is the military's way of saying to its soldiers: I know your work is difficult and dangerous, so we will give you a benefit to help make your situation bearable and profitable to you.

In a similar fashion, when God blesses a man with a wife, He is saying to the man, I know life is hard, and living by the sweat of your brow is not easy. Therefore, in order to offset the harsh brutality of life, I am going to give you a benefit, a helpmate who will provide an oasis of cool relief in what would otherwise be a hot and barren desert. Now, your oasis won't take the place of the desert; you are still going to have to face the unforgiving sun and the scorching sands. But, as you sweat, you can at least take comfort in knowing at the end of the day, there is a cool and inviting oasis waiting for you. Your oasis is there to soothe and comfort you; revive your strength; and refresh your mind, body and soul.

Wives, it is imperative you realize that you are the cool oasis your husband should think about while he's in the heat of life. God blessed your husband with you, so you could be the comfort he looks forward to enjoying. Your presence in his life should be a source of strength. It should encourage him as he wrestles with life. Even when the world around him seems to be falling apart, he should at least know he will be comforted by the love, affection, and attention of the benefits God gave him.

Imagine, therefore, the tragedy that occurs when your battle-weary husband comes home from a brutal day, and instead of an oasis of comfort, he finds more fight and heat. What a terrible irony it is when instead of being a benefit and helpmate to her husband, a wife becomes one of his tormentors; constantly telling him he doesn't measure up, constantly belittling his contribution to the family, incessantly calling into question his very manhood. In marriages where a helpmate turns into a tormentor, it is no wonder the relationship feels cursed; it is cursed. It is under the curse of being out of order.

Don't be mistaken; I am not suggesting as a wife, you are forced into silence and cannot express your concerns and even complaints about situations or objectionable behavior; however, as you express your concerns and air your grievances, you must remember the biblical admonition that everything must be done in decency and in order. This means there is not only a time and a place for the airing of grievances, but there is also a way in which it should be done. Airing grievances should not be a constant activity. Wisdom suggests, after a while, if your grievance is not duly addressed, then you need to stop complaining to your husband about it and give it over to God. Let God deal with the situation. Let go of it. Walk in peace and settle in your spirit that God has the power to change the situation without you stepping out of your role as a benefit.

Will it always be easy to do this? No. As I just outlined, sometimes it will require you to bite your tongue, table your concerns and tend to your husband's hurt, even when you are hurting. But, again, this is why God put you in your husband's life.

Being a helpmate is your divinely appointed role. And, as is the case in all roles given to us by God, to refuse the role is sinful. It is a sin for which God will hold you accountable.

Remember, no one forced you to say, "I do." By accepting his ring, you placed the burden of being a benefit upon yourself. If this is a burden you didn't want, then you should never have accepted it. But, since you have accepted it, know God will give you all the grace and strength you need to fulfill it. It may be tough at first, but as you train your heart and mind to walk in this role, it will become easier.

If your husband is godly, then he will bless you for this role. He will honor you for the contribution you make in his life. On the other hand, if your husband is not a godly man and does not show you the gratitude you deserve, then don't despair; God will pick up the slack and bless you directly. God will be prone to give you a double portion of the blessing because you are faithfully fulfilling your role as a helpmate, despite the fact your husband does not honor you for it. I have seen it time and time again, blessings that rain down on one person but not the other. A wife is blessed while her husband languishes and suffers. Her husband is barred from her blessings because they are tied to her doing what God commanded, even as her husband does not balance it out by doing what God commanded him to do.

So the bottom line is; be a benefit, be a helpmate, be an oasis in spite of for whom you are an oasis. I pray your husband will honor your comfort, but even if he does not, I know God will.

The Duties of a Wife

Be Submissive

Wives, submit yourselves unto your own husbands, as unto the lord. **Ephesians 5:22**

But I would have you know, that the head of every man is Christ; and the head of the woman [is] the man; and the head of Christ [is] God. **1 Corinthians 11:3**

Submission is, by far, the most challenging role a wife must uphold. When Bible-Believing pastors teach the biblical principle of marital submission, it often incites anger, resentment and even disbelief. The idea of a fully grown and capable woman submitting herself to a man is completely foreign to the ideals of modern society.

The fact is, most women are simply not conditioned to accept submission as a duty God expects them to fulfill. But, as the two scriptures at the beginning of this section instruct, submission is indeed the expectation God places upon wives. This expectation has neither expired nor been retracted but is as binding today as it was when it was written. You might as well face it, God wants there to be a hierarchal authority in the home, and He has placed authority in the office of the husband. Admittedly, this may not seem fair to women, but God's ways are not our ways, and His plan supersedes our limited thoughts about His plan.

In God's divine wisdom, He chose to place headship in the office of the husband as opposed to the wife. If God had chosen to do the opposite and require husbands to submit to their wives, then men would probably find this arrangement just as difficult. But, one arrangement God could not allow is to leave no one in charge and allow marriage to be completely free of headship and authority.

I often challenge those who find the idea of submission objectionable to identify one organization in which there is no system of hierarchal leadership and submission. Companies, governments, civic leagues, the military and the church all have leaders and followers. No organization or social arrangement can function without headship. Even sports teams, where players are supposedly equal members of a team, have defined leaders and followers.

The Indianapolis Colts became champions on the back of their strong leader, Peyton Manning. Even though Peyton Manning is just one member of the eleven-member team, he still functions as a leader and requires players to submit to his authority on, and sometimes off, the field. If Peyton calls a play, his teammates may disagree; but if they want to remain a Colt, then they are expected to submit.

Thus, if headship and submission are expected on something as frivolous as a football field, why wouldn't we expect to find submission at home? In a marriage where both husband and wife are calling the plays, and no one has the right to have the final say, then eventually, there's going to be a marital delay of the game, and the husband and wife will both be penalized. For this reason, God calls upon wives to acquiesce to the authority of their husbands. Furthermore, a wife must accept her husband's authority was bestowed upon him by God and should be honored.

Take comfort, wives; submission is not slavery. Just because your husband has been given authority, he does not have the right to be a tyrant. Nor does your husband have the right to devalue or ignore your input. Believe me; only a foolish man would make a decision without considering and even petitioning the input of his wife. If a husband trusts his wife to raise his kids, then he should trust her input and value her counsel. Nevertheless, when there is an impasse, or a husband feels led to go in a certain direction, **a wife is obligated to submit. There are only three exceptions to this rule. Those exceptions occur when a husband's directions are:**

Immoral

Illegal

Against the Expressed Will of God

Other than these very specific exceptions, the role of a wife is to defer to the leading authority of her husband. This rule applies even if you feel your husband doesn't deserve your submission. Remember, submission is position-based, not person-based. Since submission is position-based, you submit to your husband not because he is deserving but because he's your husband.

If this seems unreasonable to you, then you should remind yourself how faithful God is to you, in spite of what you deserve. Does God withhold His grace from you because you are undeserving of it? Does God withhold His love from you because you are undeserving of it? Since the answer to these questions is a resounding <u>NO</u>, then what gives you the right to withhold your submission because you deem your husband unworthy? If you think your husband is calling the wrong plays and he won't listen to your input, then pray for him. Don't rebel and pray; submit and pray. Believe me, God knows how to change the mind of your husband, and the prayers of a righteous woman availeth much.

So wives, submit to your husband. Submission is your reasonable and required duty. When you refuse to submit, you don't just sin against your husband; you sin against God. If you are having difficulty in this area, then pray and ask God to give you a submissive heart.

For instance, some women who have managerial authority at work have trouble relinquishing the authority when they come home. This is understandable, but it is not excusable. Your role at work should never become the predominant expression of who you are. If you are unable to reconcile your duties at work with your duties at home, then you must petition God for help. Ask God to give you the power to lead at work and submit at home.

Ask God to give you a humble heart, one that will submit to the authority of your husband. As you do this, you will gain favor, blessings and the peace that comes with knowing you are in the center of God's will for your life.

The Duties of a Wife

Be a Spiritual Supporter

In some respect, this duty is the culmination of the first two duties. This duty can also be understood as the embodiment of the adage: behind every good man, there is a great woman. I know this from personal experience.

I also know a wife who sees her life as inextricably bound with her husband's life and will do all she can to help her husband become the man God has destined him to be. By providing encouragement, support, a good home, as well as a nurturing environment, a wife has the power to thrust her husband into unimaginable success. A wife, who is a spiritual supporter of her husband, will pray for him when he falls short. She intercedes on his behalf because she knows being the head is a difficult assignment-one in which God is always judging him. I sometimes ask wives, "Have you ever considered what it must feel like being accountable to God, not just for yourself, but for another individual also?"

Sometimes, women will respond, "Of course I do; I have children." Then, I'll say to them, "Ok, but under parental authority, when a child refuses to listen, then as their mom, you can punish or spank them into compliance. But, when you, as a wife, refuse to listen, all your husband can do is talk to you, pray for you and hope you will want to comply with his authority. Hence, being accountable for someone who has the power to make their own decisions is a completely different matter; therefore, your husband needs your support, and he needs your prayers. Even if he never asks for your prayers, pray for him anyway. Pray for him as much as you pray for yourself."

And finally, I will conclude the discussion of a godly wife by offering the example found in Proverbs. The Word of God highlights the characteristics of a good and godly wife far better than a man can.

The Proverbs Woman

Proverbs 31:10-31

10A wife of noble character who can find? She is worth far more than rubies.

11Her husband has full confidence in her and lacks nothing of value.

12She brings him good, not harm, all the days of her life.

13She selects wool and flax and works with eager hands.

14She is like the merchant ships, bringing her food from afar.

15She gets up while it is still dark; she provides food for her family and portions for her servant girls.

16She considers a field and buys it; out of her earnings, she plants a vineyard.

17She sets about her work vigorously; her arms are strong for her tasks.

18She sees that her trading is profitable, and her lamp does not go out at night.

19In her hand she holds the distaff and grasps the spindle with her fingers.

20She opens her arms to the poor and extends her hands to the needy.

21When it snows, she has no fear for her household; for all of them are clothed in scarlet.

22She makes covering for her bed; she is clothed in fine linen and purple.

23Her husband is respected at the city gate, where he takes his seat among the elders of the land.

24She makes linen garments and sells them, and supplies the merchants with sashes.

25She is clothed with strength and dignity; she can laugh at the days to come.

26She speaks with wisdom, and faithful instruction is on her tongue.

27She watches over the affairs of her household and does not eat the bread of idleness.

28Her children arise and call her blessed; her husband also, and he praises her:

29"Many women do noble things, but you surpass them all."

30Charm is deceptive, and beauty is fleeting, but a woman who fears the LORD is to be praised.

31Give her the reward she has earned, and let her works bring her praise at the city gate.

The Duties of a Husband

Ok, husbands, now it's your turn. I am sure that you wholeheartedly agreed with the duties of a wife, shaking your head in approval and taking notes. Before you celebrate, you should know that the reason I outlined the duties of a wife first is that I saved the most difficult assignment for last. Oh yes, the duties of a godly husband are numerous and more exacting than the duties of a wife.

Husbands, because you are the head, God places a heavier burden on you. He expects and requires more of you. To borrow a phrase from President Harry Truman, "the buck stops with you." This means your wife, her welfare, her honor, and even her growth and development are your responsibility. This realization became abundantly clear to me on my wedding day.

I'll never forget that day; the room was full of well-wishers. There I stood, with the preacher, waiting for the Wedding March to begin and for my beautiful bride to make her grand entrance and walk down the aisle. As the music started to play and I saw her enter the room, I felt proud and confident. There was no fear in me. I didn't have the slightest bit of hesitation; I was enjoying my wedding day. But, when my wife made it halfway down the aisle, the preacher, with base and authority in his voice, turned to me and said, "Turn around and face your responsibility."

"What!?" My heart jumped. I thought to myself, I know I didn't just hear what I thought I heard. I must have misunderstood what the preacher just told me. After all, that is my wife, not my responsibility. This preacher is trippin'. The wise preacher didn't back down, though. Without hesitation, the preacher repeated himself, this time loud enough to make sure everyone heard his instruction, "Turn around and face your responsibility."

At that very moment, the magnitude of what I was about to do came crashing down on me like a ton of bricks. I thought, *am I really ready for this? I want a wife, not a responsibility.*

As I was standing there thinking about this, all my confidence and bravado faltered; suddenly, I felt nervous and unsure. And to make matters worse, the preacher wasn't finished. He had more to say, "That's right, son, go on and get your responsibility and walk her down here with you."

So, that's just what I did. Scared and nervous, I walked up the aisle, took my responsibility by the hand, brought her to me and married her. That day I vowed before God and man to keep that responsibility unto death do us part.

What a revelation. The preacher's words are just as heavy today as they were on my wedding day. My wife is my responsibility. This means it is my duty as her husband to care for her spiritually, mentally, physically, emotionally and financially. I may have been given headship over her, but I can never forget that to whom much is given, much is required.

Husbands, prepare yourself as I lay out what is required of you. The duties of a husband are:

Be a Leader

Be a Provider

Maintain Your Wife's Honor

Be a Family Man

<u>BE A LEADER</u>

Your most important task is to lead. If you want your wife to fulfill her role of submission, then you must provide leadership. If you expect her to follow, then she expects you to lead. And contrary to what you may believe, leadership doesn't mean you stand on the sidelines barking orders or climb on top of your high horse and throw down edicts like a king. True leadership takes the form of leading by example or servant-leadership.

Your wife and your family are a reflection of you. If you are mean, dishonest, carnal, hurtful and vindictive, then over time, your family will adopt these same attributes and character flaws. However, if you are faithful, caring, kind and compassionate, then your family will eventually catch on and join you in your honorable state.

You may have to face the unpleasant truth that if your wife has severe shortcomings, then her shortcomings are symptomatic of a failure in leadership. Although most men are reluctant to take responsibility for their wife's deficiencies, the truth is we are responsible. Certainly not in every case, but in many cases, the reason wives fall short in following is that their husbands have fallen short in leading. Furthermore, the reason wives are out of order is that day in and day out, they constantly see their husbands act out of order. Consider the story of Mr. and Mrs. Rush. They are at the supermarket. Mr. Rush is in a hurry; he wants to get home in time to see the big game. His mission is to grab a few items, rush home and be in front of the TV in time for the kickoff.

Mr. Rush hurries down each aisle, checking his watch. He knows he's cutting it close but figures he'll make it home in time because he's almost done. However, when Mr. and Mrs. Rush reach the checkout lanes, to their dismay, they discover just a few lanes are open. Worse yet, the lanes are backed up with shoppers whose carts are filled with groceries.

"This is ridiculous," Mr. Rush mumbles to himself. Unwilling to concede defeat, Mr. Rush looks towards the express lane. He grins in delight when he sees the express lane is open, and there is nobody in it.

When he starts to head for the express lane, his wife grabs his arm, "Honey," she says, "we have too many items for the express lane. Let's just stay here."

Undeterred by his wife's admonishment, Mr. Rush heads towards the express lane anyway. Once there, he begins to quickly unload his cart onto the conveyor. When the cashier looks up and sees all the items coming toward her, she points to the sign and politely tells Mr. Rush he has to use the regular lane because he has too many items for the express lane.

Now here comes the moment of leadership failure. Instead of being an example of orderly behavior and modeling godly submission, Mr. Rush becomes irate. Right there in front of his wife, he starts arguing with the young cashier about how silly she's being. And, since no one is behind them, he asks her why she's making such a big deal about how many items he has. He then proceeds to place the rest of his items on the conveyer and advises the cashier he's not switching lines, so she might as well hurry up and check him out.

Meanwhile, Mrs. Rush is standing by watching her husband make a mockery of the store's rules and the cashier's authority. Although no words are ever exchanged between husband and wife, nonetheless, through his childish behavior, Mr. Rush is telling his wife that it's ok to rebel against authority.

Mr. Rush will go home, watch the big game and never give his behavior a second thought. Even as he sits in front of his pastor two weeks later to complain about his wife and lament the fact that his wife doesn't respect his authority, he never stops to reflect upon his leadership failures. Mr. Rush doesn't see how he is merely reaping what he has sown. Seemingly meaningless interactions, like the one at the grocery store, have all come home to roost. Mr. Rush has no one to blame but himself.

The lesson of this story is to point out how crucial it is that a husband leads his wife by setting a good example. Never lose sight of the fact your wife is watching you and being influenced by what you do and how you do it.

Also, be sure to make the connection between how you treat others and how your wife will treat you. When you disrespect your boss, your pastor, or even the cashier behind the counter, you will eventually reap the same disrespect. How you respond to others' authority determines how your wife responds to your authority. Therefore, be a leader. Do the right thing and model godly behavior for your family. Give them a standard to which they can reach. Show them you are not only able to talk-the-talk, but more importantly, you can walk-the-walk. Just as faith without works is dead, submission without leadership is also dead.

I should also point out that leadership involves courage. I see too many men who are so hen-pecked and scared they cannot even lead the family dog. Fear is counterproductive to leadership. The fear of being disliked, the fear of making someone angry, the fear of conflict, all of these fears will destroy your ability to lead. If you cannot stand up and do what is right, even in the face of adversity, then you cannot lead. If you are more afraid of disappointing your wife than you are of disappointing God, then you cannot lead. You might as well accept that sometimes when you make a tough decision, it will cause conflict and tension. That's why you need to develop courage and possess the strength of your convictions. Rebuke the spirit of fear and walk in your calling as a man.

The final dimension of leadership is leadership demands love. The Bible instructs husbands to love their wives, as Christ loves the church. The implication is that your leadership must be rooted in love. When love is the foundation of your leadership, your wife's needs are more important than your own needs. Moreover, your criteria for making decisions will be what is best for your wife, as opposed to what is best for you.

Also, while love-based leadership is strong and resolute, it is never mean, selfish or abusive (mentally, physically, emotionally or verbally). Love-based leadership builds up and does not tear down. It promotes forgiveness and not retaliation. Just as Christ's love-based leadership over us works to our benefit, your loved-based leadership should work to your wife's benefit.

BE A PROVIDER

A husband's job is to care for his wife and to make sure her needs are met. A husband is spiritually mandated to provide his wife and family with food, shelter, clothing, transportation, as well as social and educational needs. Even if his wife works and is able to contribute to the household and to her own care, this does not mean he is off the hook for being the one who is ultimately responsible for taking care of her. If, for whatever reason, his wife stops working or is unable to work, he needs to be prepared to assume the role of the family's sole provider.

This, of course, means a godly husband must have a strong work ethic. Being the head of the house means you should either be working or actively looking for work. If working one job doesn't produce enough income to make ends meet, then work two jobs. If two jobs aren't enough, then work three jobs. You may even have to go back to school to learn a new trade and gain new skills in order to position yourself to be a good provider. As long as it's legal and moral, do whatever you have to do to keep food on the table, clothes on her back, a roof over her head, gas in her car and so on. Anything less than this means you are not honoring your commitment.

> *If anyone does not provide for his relatives and*
> *especially for immediate family he has denied*
> *the faith and is worse than an unbeliever.*
> *1 Timothy 5:8*

Any man who doesn't want to bear this kind of responsibility has no business taking on a wife. Once you become a husband, then slacking off is not an option. Being lazy, slothful, unambitious or unconcerned about the welfare of your family is sinful and a violation of your God-given role as the head of the house. When the family's needs are not met, you shoulder the blame. The buck stops with you.

It is worth pointing out; however, there is a difference between needs and desires. Being a provider does not mean you must provide a lavish or luxurious lifestyle. If God blesses you to be able to enjoy the finer things in life, then, by all means, spoil your wife and reap the benefits of your prosperity.

On the other hand, if you are working as hard as you can and making wise financial decisions but still have limited resources, then that's ok. Hopefully, before you married your wife, she saw you for who you were and not for whom she wanted you to be. A woman who marries a garbage collector, who lives a modest life, has no right to expect to live as though she married Bill Gates. God is just as pleased with the hardworking man who provides an apartment for his family as He is with the man who is able to give his family a house on a hill.

Just be faithful in providing that apartment and keep on working in the hopes one day, God will open a door, so you can improve your lot in life. When your wife sees you striving to build a better life, she'll have the hope of a brighter tomorrow.

In the same vein, make sure, even in your limited means, every once in a while, you splurge on your wife and show her in tangible ways you appreciate her. You may not be able to meet all of her desires, but you should strive to meet at least some of them. Being a good provider requires wisdom in knowing when to hold back and when to be liberal.

As a husband, you must do everything, legal and moral, to provide for your wife. Your wife is your charge, and you must take care of her. She is not her parent's responsibility, her family's responsibility or her own responsibility-she is your responsibility.

MAINTAIN YOUR WIFE'S HONOR

In the section on leadership, I asserted a wife is a reflection of her husband. Now, I want to go a step further and suggest a husband is a reflection of his wife. Being a reflection of your wife signifies that her honor will become your honor, or her dishonor will become your dishonor. A husband who understands this will do everything in his power to protect his wife from anything that threatens her virtue, dignity, character and reputation. He will make sure he never brings shame upon his wife or his home. He pays his bills on time, makes sure the cars and the home are in good shape, keeps his reputation beyond reproach and never gives anyone just cause to question his love and devotion for his family.

By keeping the stain of scandals far away from the marriage cup, you allow your wife to walk around town with her head held high. She becomes a woman of honor in a world full of dishonored women. Her honor will produce peace, confidence and gracefulness in her deportment. She will be beautifully adorned with virtue. When she walks by your side, radiating poise and distinction, you will bask in its glow and reap the benefits of protecting her honor.

<u>BE A FAMILY MAN</u>

Once a man accepts the responsibility of a wife and the possibility of children, he loses the right to spend his free time in any way he chooses. The bulk of your free time will become family time. There will still be opportunities to hang out with friends and play a round of golf, but these extracurricular activities should never threaten home life.

The responsibility of raising a family and being a husband comes first. Tragedies occur when children grow up without the love and attention of their dads. They become love-starved and may spend their entire life trying to fill the void caused by an absentee father who was too busy with his own life. Being a family man mandates you give your wife and children the attention they need to feel loved.

Being a family man also requires you to participate in the life of the home. Don't be fooled into thinking it's your wife's job to do all the chores around the house and raise the kids by herself, when all you have to do is bring home a paycheck and relax. The truth is, you have an obligation to pitch in and help your wife. It's your duty to relieve your wife and lessen her load. If she looks burned out by the chores of life, then don't just stand around expecting her to recover on her own, help her recover by giving her a break and picking up the slack.

Every man should know how to cook, clean, do laundry, change a diaper and all the other tasks that usually fall on a wife. Nowadays, most women work a full-time job, just like their husbands. Since they are working outside the home, it isn't fair to expect them to do all the work at home. Moreover, placing this kind of burden on your wife isn't healthy for the relationship. It breeds bitterness and contempt. Show your wife you love her by helping out. You will be surprised at what a positive difference this will make in your marriage.

A Final Word on Roles

The roles and duties listed above are an overview. In addition to these gender-specific duties, there are, of course, duties that both husband and wife must fulfill. Being respectful of one another, refraining from using hurtful and derogatory speech, being faithful, supporting each other in sickness and in health, and living up to your wedding vows are also duties God expects you to fulfill.

Conclusion

Joy in the Cup

By reading this book, you have demonstrated to God and yourself how serious you are about maintaining your spiritual covenant. I'm sure there were portions of this book that challenged you. You may even have had some of your long-held beliefs and positions turned upside down. Being challenged in this way is never pleasurable. Sometimes the most difficult endeavor in life is to hear and accept the truth. As the saying goes, sometimes the truth hurts. But the truth also sets you free.

By taking the time to learn the biblical principles of marriage, you set yourself up for a blessing of joy and happiness. The joy you will experience is not new joy, it's the joy that has been in your marriage cup all along. The only reason you may not have tasted it in its fullness is due to strife and bitterness in your cup. By removing all the contaminants, you will be able to take a long refreshing sip of unpolluted sweetness and goodness.

So, if your marriage is already strong, then make it even stronger. And, if your marriage is in trouble, don't give up. Pray and ask God to restore the joy in your cup!

Definition of Marriage

Marriage is a

Divine Institution

created by God

whereby a rational

Male and Female,

who are born again,

choose to enter into

a covenant relationship

with each other

and have made an unconditional,

lifetime commitment

to God

to stay with an

imperfect person

for the rest of

their natural life.

Made in the USA
Middletown, DE
18 November 2024

64826519R00055